Color, Craft & Doodle
is all about cats—and you!

Use your imagination as you fill-in, add-to, color, and create whatever you like and wherever you like. Of course, you might have to paws when a certain furry friend decides to take a nap in the middle of the page!

I am a *CAT*
and I do as *I please*—
Like ambush the mouse
and nibble *its cheese.*
I worry *the fish*
whenever *I wish,*
And I might *take my nap*
on your *dinner dish.*
Yes, *I am a CAT*—
And THAT is THAT!

As any cat-lover knows...

- Among your many cat-friendly friends, there's one who really prefers to remain cat-free. That's the one person's lap your cat jumps on as soon as she sits down.

- If you leave your black jacket on your bed, that's where your white cat will sleep all afternoon.

- Let the cat outside, and she'll want to come inside. Let her inside, and she'll stand at the door until you let her outside.

- Remove the throws and blankets covering your sofa, and a hairball will soon be deposited on the cushion.

- No matter how many times you remove a cat from the kitchen counter, he'll jump back up (whether or not he really wants to be there).

- Whenever kitty manages to sneak a chicken wing from the kitchen, she takes it directly to your white-carpeted bedroom to eat.

- Open your morning newspaper, and across the centerfold is where your cat will choose to lie.

Never
stop
looking up...
You're sure
to see
God's love
shining down.

"Cats with Flower Bucket" Design

Colored By: ______________________________

Date: ___________________________________

Cat Crazy Word Search

There are all kinds of cats and cat-related words hidden in this puzzle! See how quickly you can pounce on all of them. Words can read to the right or left, diagonally or vertically.

Bobtail	Feline	Meow	Rug	Tiger
Calico	Finicky	Nap	Siamese	Tom
Catnip	Kitten	Panther	Striped	Treats
Claws	Lap	Play	Tabby	
Cougar	Lion	Puma	Tail	

O	K	L	M	D	E	P	I	R	T	S
N	E	I	A	C	C	O	M	S	E	T
S	E	L	T	A	B	B	Y	W	M	A
A	P	A	N	T	H	E	R	A	E	E
F	E	L	I	N	E	L	A	L	O	R
I	C	I	N	I	A	N	O	C	W	T
N	T	O	M	P	A	N	I	L	O	U
I	A	N	T	A	I	L	L	A	S	T
C	B	O	B	T	A	I	L	M	P	I
K	E	D	O	C	L	N	U	R	U	G
Y	E	S	I	A	M	E	S	E	M	E
S	Y	A	L	P	C	O	U	G	A	R

I think I'll take a little nap... fourteen or fifteen hours should do it.

The other cat says,
"Doctor, what are you working on today?"
The first cat answers,
"My usual...String Theory."

Cat Crazy Word Search Solution

O	K	L	M	D	E	P	I	R	T	S
N	E	I	A	C	C	O	M	S	E	T
S	E	L	T	A	B	B	Y	W	M	A
A	P	A	N	T	H	E	R	A	E	E
F	E	L	I	N	E	L	A	L	O	R
I	C	I	N	I	A	N	O	C	W	T
N	T	O	M	P	A	N	I	L	O	U
I	A	N	T	A	I	L	L	A	S	T
C	B	O	B	T	A	I	L	M	P	I
K	E	D	O	C	L	N	U	R	U	G
Y	E	S	I	A	M	E	S	E	M	E
S	Y	A	L	P	C	O	U	G	A	R

"And the problem is...?"

Attitude
is
everything.

Choose
happiness.

"Feline and Fountain" Design

Colored By: ______________________________

Date: ____________________________________

WHEN GOD MADE CATS

When God made cats,
he used the graceful
waving of the grass,
The gentle murmur of the river
as its waters pass,
The happy flight of butterflies
that dart among the flowers,
The peaceful, dreamy quality
of quiet nighttime hours.

When God made cats,
he took the warmth
of sunshine in the spring,
The bright and joyful sound of robins
as they chirp and sing,
He added love and faithfulness
through all the nights and days,
And made a creature who is simply
perfect in all ways!

How to Draw a Cat

1. Start by creating oval shapes to show the cat's pose.

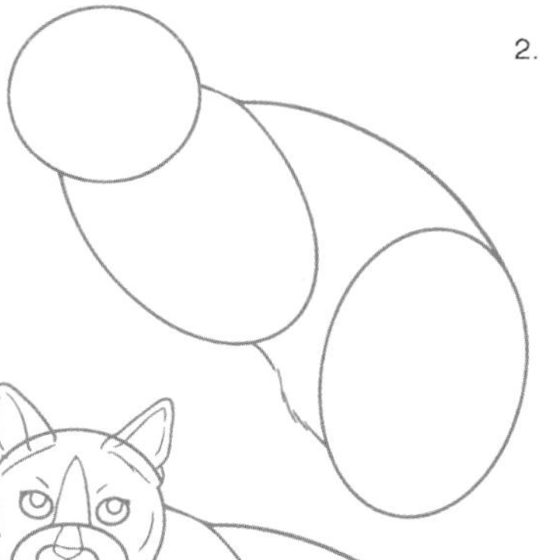

2. Draw two triangular shapes for the ears, add ovals for the muzzle and eyes. Add curved lines for the tail.

3. Continue creating the cat by adding facial details, ovals for paws, curved lines for the legs.

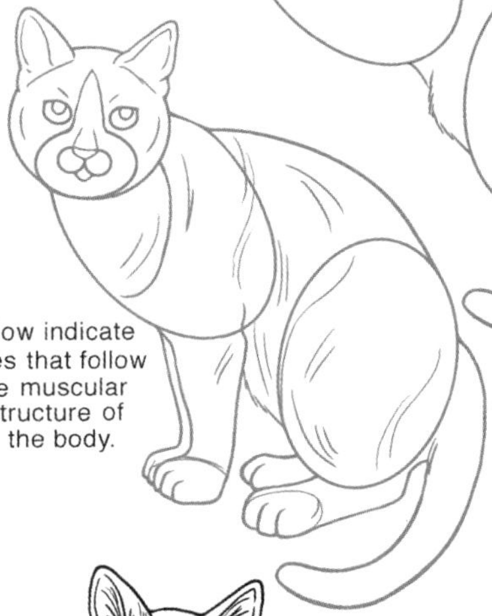

4. Now indicate lines that follow the muscular structure of the body.

5. Eliminate first rough sketched lines as your drawing becomes more cat like.

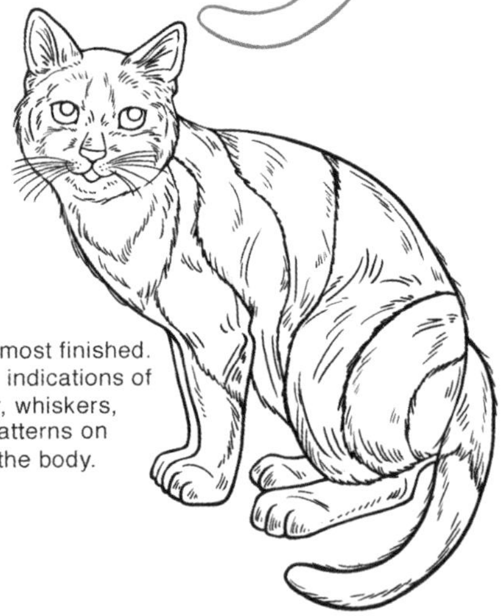

6. Almost finished. Add indications of fur, whiskers, patterns on the body.

You never know what you might find in the garden... perhaps a little patch of heaven on earth.

"Patch of Heaven" Design

Colored By: ______________________________

Date: ____________________________________

Purrfectly Expressive!

The expression, the cat's pajamas, originated in the 1920s during the jazz age. A cat—a cool person—and pajamas—a new fashion in women's nightwear—combined to refer to something totally pawsome!

"Cat got your tongue?" Most of us of a certain age may have heard that question from a parent or teacher when we were children. It meant that an answer was expected, despite our reluctance to come up with one. The origin of the idiom is unknown.

Why does it rain "cats and dogs" and not, say, lions and tigers? No one knows for sure! Some etymologists suggest that the centuries-old expression originated in Scandinavia, Greece, or England.

The "fat cat" isn't necessarily the feline that likes her food served in double or triple portions, but refers to a very wealthy person. The expression is often used disparagingly, due to its roots in 1920s politics, where the "fat cat" was a campaign contributor who hoped to buy influence and advantage in government.

When the cat's away, the mice will play! This phrase can be traced back to 15th century England. Apparently the tendency to take it easy when the teacher (or the boss) steps out of the room is nothing new!

THE WORLD ACCORDING TO CATS

Always take time for a pet-icure.

"Insomnia? I can't even spell it."

"I wish I could, but Mom says I can't come out and play with you—ever!"

"For your safety, I have to confiscate your fishsticks."

"This is how I get around when my humans aren't looking."

KITTY'S BEDTIME PRAYER

Now I lay me down to sleep,
I pray this cushy life to keep.
I pray for toys that look like mice,
and sofa cushions, soft and nice.
For grocery bags where I can hide,
just like a tiger, crouched inside!
I pray for gourmet Kitty snacks,
and someone nice to scratch my back.
For window sills all warm and bright,
for shadows to explore at night.
I pray I'll always stay real cool,
and keep the secret feline rule
To NEVER tell a human that...
the world is really ruled by CATS!

Author Unknown

NEVER
tell a
human that...
the world
is really ruled
by CATS!

"Kitty's Bedtime Prayer" Design

Colored By: ______________________________

Date: ______________________________

Career Cats

FIRST AID Kit
CatAMARAN PILOT
ASTROCat
MEWS REPURRTER
KATT TV
COPYCat
Litter CARRIER
PurrSONAL TRAINER
U CAN DO IT
ABC
123
EDUCatER
MAIL

A Cat Lives Here

Furry ball
Of warmth and grace,
Amber eyes
On whiskered face.
Zany larks,
Frenzied glare—
Languid prowl
To comfy chair.
Hear the purr?
Me-ew, me-ew!
There's a cat
At home with you!

Everybody
deserves
their
own
"happy place."

"Tiger on a Tapestry" Design

Colored By: ______________________________

Date: ____________________________________

Caption This...

These Kitties Rock!

Add a little whimsy to your patio or garden with rock kitties. Smooth, flat rocks work best. Each kitty needs one large oval rock for the body; a smaller round rock for the head; two small pointed rocks for the ears, and pebbles for the whiskers and tail. Arrange rocks on a flat surface to create a sitting cat or a walking cat. With pebbles, form whiskers and tail. It's that easy!

At a craft store, buy a shadow box or wooden box and glue. (Optional: Paint the frame or box as desired.) Arrange your rock kitty in the shadow box or on the lid of the wooden box, and secure with glue. It will add a purrfect touch to your home—or tickle the heart of a cat-loving friend!

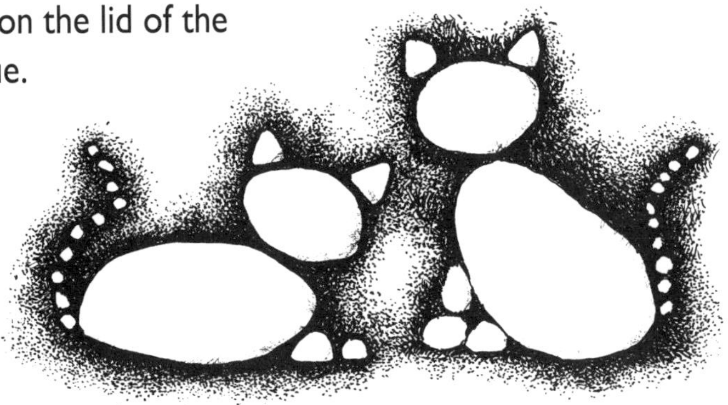

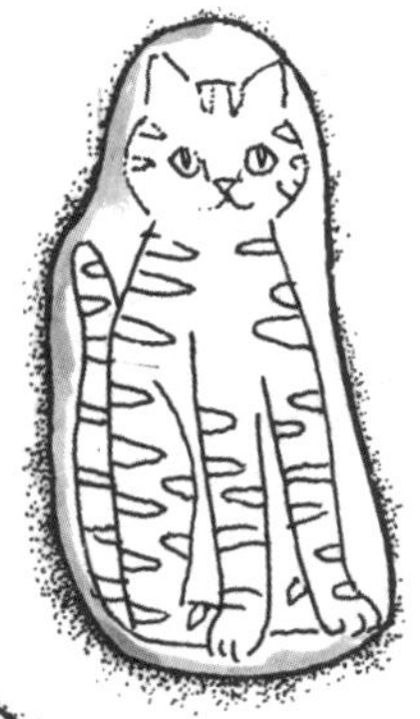

Paint a rock!

Find a small flat smooth rock and let the shape inspire your cat image. Use permanent markers or acrylic paint to design. Place these fun rocks in your own garden, or hide them in other spaces to surprise and delight those who discover them!

Bless Them All,
Dear Lord

Hear our prayer, Lord, for all animals...
May they be well-fed
and well-treated and happy;
Protect them from hunger
and fear and suffering.
And, we pray,
protect especially, dear Lord,
the little Cat who
is the companion
of our home –
Keep her safe
as she goes out,
And bring her back
to comfort us.
Amen

Protect
especially,
dear Lord,
the little Cat
who is the
companion
of our home.

"Bless Them All" Design

Colored By: ______________________________

Date: ______________________________

Paws to Connect the Dots

Solution on next page.

Paws to Connect the Dots Solution

Beauty
may be said
to be God's
trademark
in
creation.

Henry Ward Beecher

"Surrounded by Butterflies" Design

Colored By: ______________________________

Date: ____________________________________

Cat Meowjis

You'll never guess what I just did!

Honestly, do you think I'm going to play with that stupid toy?

Your vet knows nothing about good food!

The salmon was tasty—I even left a little for your dinner guests.

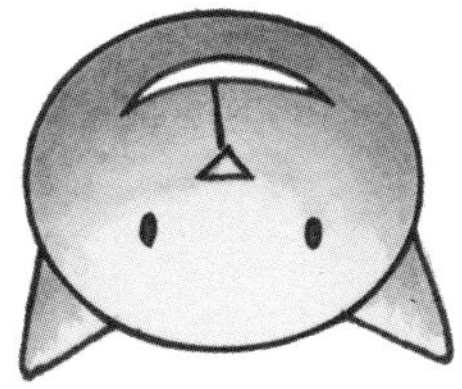

Hey, this chandelier has a lot of swing to it!

Who, me?

I'm about to go bonkers for no apparent reason.

Obviously fake! Real cats don't do applause.

Feline Feelings for You

Cats, unlike dogs, aren't known for their responsiveness to human emotions. Yet recent studies have indicated what most cat-companions already know—cats sense how we're feeling. It's thought that they pick up on our facial expressions, and over time become quite attuned to our moods. So when you feel happy, your cat feels happy, too (and happier yet when you reach for her favorite treat)!

A PURRRFECT DAY IN THE LIFE OF A CAT

"Kittens and Rosebuds" Design

Colored By: ______________________________

Date: ___________________________________

Cat Quips & Quotes

I never cry over spilled milk—or spilled anything, for that matter.

I think I'll pamper myself today…and tomorrow…and the next day…

Guaranteed—she'll never find where I hid those cat toys!

They say that dogs have owners and cats have staff. It's so true.

If you own a kitten, life overflows with Cuteness.

Enjoy each day, knowing how much you're loved and admired…
at least by your cat.

THE WORLD ACCORDING TO

Major catastrophe - Dinner is five minutes late!

Bed - Wherever you happen to lie down and take a nap.

Over-stuffed sofa - Scratching post

Christmas tree - Playtime!!

Tasty snack - Leaves of the exotic houseplant your humans thought you couldn't reach—huh!

Vet's waiting room - Best place to screech as loudly and as irritatingly as possible.

Kitty toys - Do-dads humans seem to enjoy dangling in front of you, but, honestly, they're sooo borrrring.

Bath water - Claw time!

RELATIONSHIP ADVICE FROM A WISE CAT:

Sometimes it's best to just hiss and make up.

Kitty Kitty?...

Paws to Ponder

Have you ever tried herding cats? It's next to impossible, given their independent nature! We humans might take a tip from our feline friends—instead of blindly going along with the crowd, make sure the crowd is going where we want to end up!

A time for feathers, balls, and catnip mice—and a time to take a nap in a quiet, comfy corner. Leave a peaceful space in your day when your electronic devices are on silent mode. Do like a cat and take a nap! It's a purrfect pick-me-up in a hectic day.

A cat doesn't need words to express her affection. You know it by the nose-rubs against your face, the kneading paws in your lap, and the soft rumble of a deep, contented purr. Let the people you love know how you feel not just by the words you speak, but by the things you do.

ACROSS

1 "It's sure __ to chase 5-Down around a little!!"
4 Roman cats' debate venue
6 "That's an ancestor of mine--the big guy."
7 Human's best response to cat's demand
9 Cat of many years
10 French affirmation
11 Afternoon nap time (Abbr.)
12 Corrode, like metal
13 "It's something to lick off my human's dinner plate."
15 "She says this every time I bring her something from outside."

DOWN

1 "Put it in my bowl—now!"
2 Large metal container with a tap
3 Greek alphabet
4 "The great ones put cats in starring roles."
5 House rodent
6 Snip
8 Newborn cat
10 "One little claw scratch, and this is what she says!"
12 Convenient cat scratching item
14 Gold (Abbr.)

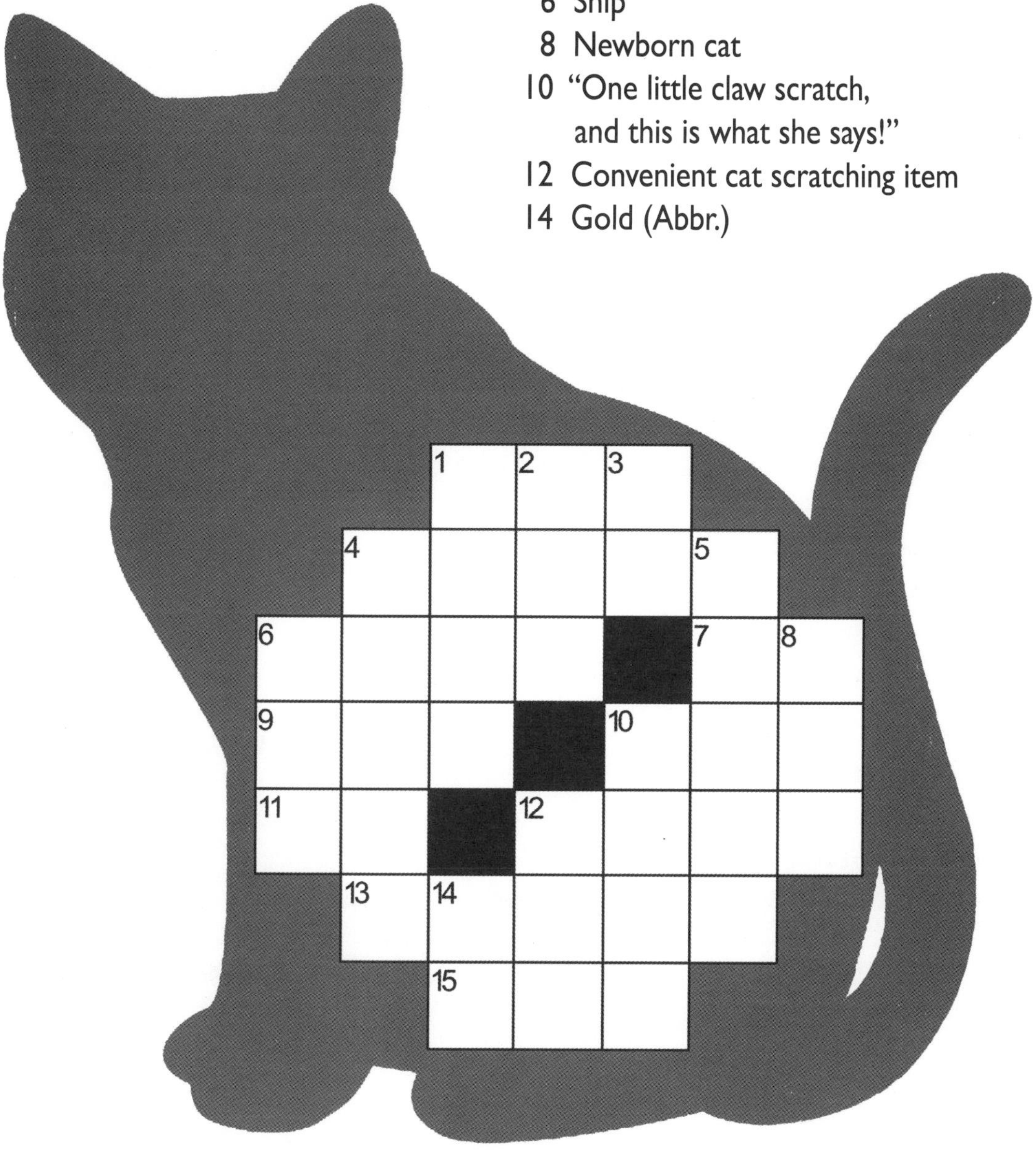

Some Important Things I've Learned From My Cat

Enjoy the present moment.
It won't last long, and it will never come again.

Slow down, relax, take a nap now and then.
It's a good way to refresh the mind and reenergize the body.

Take time to play. It will keep you feeling young.

Any time you have requests or opinions,
state them politely, but firmly.

If you aren't heard the first time, repeat yourself until you are!

Make one chair your special favorite and revisit it often.

Show your affection openly. There's nothing like a little purring and closeness to alleviate stress.

When it comes to food,
always show yourself to be a
true connoisseur.

Try to spend some time each day
keeping yourself clean and neatly groomed.

Never lose your sense of curiosity.
There is a whole world out there,
just waiting to be explored.

Paws to Ponder Solution

		1 F	2 U	3 N		
	4 F	O	R	U	5 M	
6 L	I	O	N	■	7 O	8 K
9 O	L	D	■	10 O	U	I
11 P	M	■	12 R	U	S	T
	13 S	14 A	U	C	E	
		15 U	G	H		

I'M A CAT

I'm only a cat,
and I stay in my place-
Up there on your chair,
on your bed or your face!
I'm only a cat,
and I don't finicky much-
I'm happy with cream
and anchovies and such!
I'm only a cat,
and we'll get along fine,
As long as you know
I'm not yours-you're all mine!

Author Unknown

I'm only a cat,
and we'll get
along fine,
As long as you
know I'm
not yours-
you're all mine!

"Happy Cat Border" Design

Colored By: ______________________________

Date: ____________________________________

Caption This...

I'll Do It My Way, Thanks...

The smallest feline is a masterpiece.

Leonardo da Vinci

"Beautiful Cat with Butterfly Garden" Design

Colored By: ______________________________

Date: ___________________________________

A cat
pours his
body on
the floor
like water.
It is restful
just to see him.
William Lyon Phelps

"Cat On Rug" Design

Colored By: ______________________________

Date: __________________________________

Follow the color key on the back cover for this color-by-number design, or create your own original color scheme

Caption This...

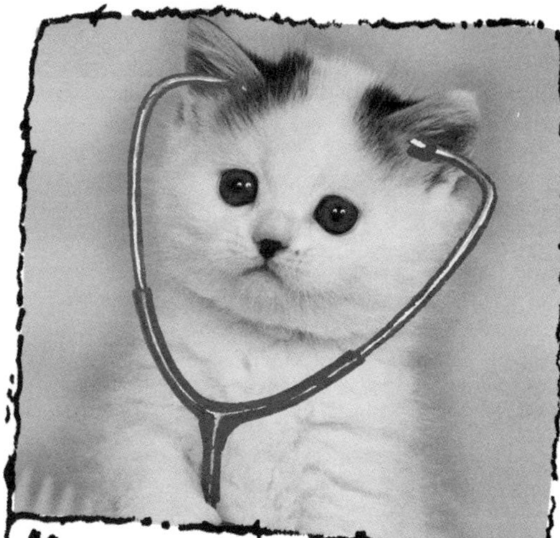

RULES FOR THE CAT

1. The cat may sleep on the bed, but only on the foot of the bed.
2. Okay, the cat is allowed to sleep up against the human, but not on the pillow.
3. The cat can sleep on the pillow, but definitely not on the human's face.
4. Fine! The human will adjust his or her sleeping position to accommodate the comfort of the cat.
5. The cat is allowed on the furniture, but not during shedding season.
6. Okay, the cat can shed on the furniture, but no claws will be sharpened there.
7. Very well, the human will invest in expensive scratching posts and plan on replacing the furniture periodically.
8. The cat may jump on the kitchen counter, but not while food is being prepared.
9. All right, the cat can be on the counter during food preparation, but must maintain a respectful distance at all times.
10. "Respectful distance" means farther than one inch!
11. The cat is definitely not allowed on the dining room table.
12. Well, okay, but not during meals.
13. No! No! The cat will not eat off the human's plate!

RULES FOR THE HUMAN

1. The human needs to learn that making rules for a cat is impossible!

Where's Kitty?

There's a feline hiding in each sentence—can you spot her? The first one is done for you!

Tabby	Ragdoll	Tiger
Calico	Leopard	Angora
Panther	Bengal	Puma

1. Pull the tab by the door!

2. "It's an anti-germ spray," she told me.

3. "Ben, gallop!" shouted the stallion's rider.

4. The bridge will span the river here.

5. Leo, pardon me, are you taking in gerbils?

6. Rum-pa-pa-pum—a drum sounded in the distance.

7. "It's medical," I commented to the passerby.

8. "Sweetie, you mustn't drag dollies by their hair!"

9. It was like a pang or an ache.

Answers on next page.

Puzzle Solution

WHERE'S KITTY?

1. Pull the **TAB BY** the door!

2. "It's an an**TI-GER**m spray," she told me.

3. "**BEN, GAL**lop!" shouted the stallion's rider.

4. The bridge will s**PAN THE R**iver here.

5. **LEO, PARD**on me, are you taking in gerbils?

6. Rum-pa-pa-**PUM—A** drum sounded in the distance.

7. "It's medi**CAL," I CO**mmented to the passerby.

8. "Sweetie, you mustn't d**RAG DOLL**ies by their hair!"

9. It was like a p**ANG OR A**n ache.

You can never see the world all at once,
so just open your eyes really big
and take in as much
as possible.

Author Unknown

All animals,
except man,
know that
the principal
business of
life is to
enjoy it.

Samuel Butler

"In His Domain" Design

Colored By: ______________________________

Date: ______________________________

Paws to Connect the Dots

Solution on next page.

Paws to Connect the Dots Solution

The journey is always nicer when you're walking side-by-side with a friend.

There are 9 differences between these two pictures—can you find them all?

Solution on next page.

It's a Feline World

Keyboards are for sleeping,
Stairways are for naps...
Your cell phone is for adding
Funny kitten apps.

TP in the bathroom
Is for feline kicks...
All food on kitchen counters
Gets a few good licks.

Curtains hang for climbing,
Carpets spread to shred...
And any chair you sit on,
Off! It's now my bed!

Yes, each and every morning,
You can clearly see
The grand old sun arising
Just to shine on me!

A well-spent day brings happy sleep.
Leonardo da Vinci

Differences Solution: 1) Blade of grass added on sidewalk 2) Tree trunk on left longer 3) Pine tree on left moved 4) Hill added in background 5) Striped cat front paw moved 6) Kitty moved forward 7) Blade of grass removed in front of house 8) Window bigger 9) Bird added on top of house

"I Am The Cat–

you are the lowly human."

~The Cat

Life According to Dogs, Life According to Cats

Kitty Page Peeper

Doesn't the cat always want to be on top of whatever you're reading? Here's a clever bookmark to make for yourself, or for a cat-loving friend.

You will need:

- 3x5 index card, or heavy weight paper
- Close-up photo of your cat's head
- Glue
- Scissors

1. Glue a photo of your cat to an index card.

2. Cut around the cat's head, then cut straight down to the bottom of the card, leaving space under kitty's image.

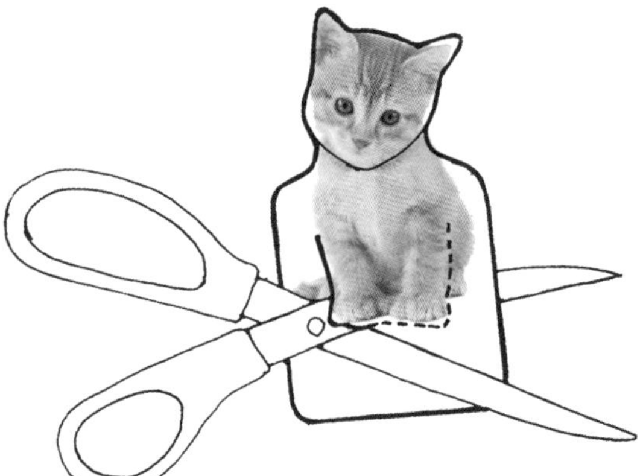

3. Carefully cut a slit around the paws.

4. It should look something like this when done!

5. Mark your spot by attaching to the top of the page!

Animals
are such
agreeable friends–
they ask
no questions;
they pass
no criticisms.

George Eliot

"Rocking Chair" Design

Colored By: ______________________________

Date: ____________________________________

A cat knows...sometimes the best thing to do is nothing at all.

There are 9 differences between these two pictures—can you find them all?

Solution on next page.

There is
no snooze
button
on a cat
who wants
breakfast.

Differences Solution: 1) Lamp base moved 2) Cat on chair, tail repositioned 3) Chair arm wing is smaller 4) Bird moved 5) Cat in window smaller 6) Picture smaller 7) Outlet moved 8) Stripped cat moved 9) Drapes shortened

THE WORLD'S MOST PURRFECT CAT

All kinds of cats make purrfect friends,
whatever color, shape, or size—
A cuddly-nuzzly ball of fur,
a whiskered, winsome, paw-some prize!

They're quick to make themselves at home
and occupy your favorite chair—
And if you'd like to sit there, too,
the feline might agree to share.

While some are quite persnickety,
some other cats are more laidback—
But all will thrive when served with love,
(and few would spurn a midnight snack).

From kitten-sweet to tomcat-tough,
each cat is mew-y, mew-y fine—
But I can say without a doubt,
The world's most purrfect cat is MINE!

There's Something About Cats

Words in this puzzle are all about our feline friends!

ACROSS

2 A feral cat is this.
7 The cat who's checking out her new toy is this.
8 All cats are this, you must agree!
10 Cats that walk across a mantel without knocking anything down are this.
12 This often described the physique of a Siamese cat.
15 The cat that likes to be held is this.
16 The ___ cat can easily jump from sofa to shelf.
17 Cats spend a lot of time grooming themselves; they're very ___.
18 Cats are generally ___, except when they want you to serve dinner—now!
19 If your cat catches a mouse and brings it to you, she's feeling ___!

DOWN

1 If a tabby has this color stripes, it's usually a tom.
3 Playful kittens are this.
4 Cats can be ___ to respond to you...when they want to!
5 Here's a word to describe a street-wise tomcat!
6 Kittens romping together are this.
9 Like 15 Down, this word often describes kittens.
11 A cozy, curled-up purring cat is this.
13 Long-hair cats are this.
14 A tri-colored cat is this.
15 All kittens are this--they just can't help it!

Solution on next page.

If humans were more like cats, we would…

…look at our world with fresh eyes every morning.

…take pleasure in sunbeams, leaves, and butterflies.

…watch patiently for opportunities, then pounce on them.

…be a little less concerned about winning the approval of others.

…find our bliss in a soft, comfy chair.

There's Something About Cats Solution

Everything that moves serves to interest and amuse a cat.

F A Paradis de Moncrif

"Beautiful Butterfly Watcher" Design

Colored By: ______________________________

Date: ___________________________________

Cat and Mouse Maze

Help the mouse scamper to the safety of his house in the middle of the maze!

Solution on next page.

cute cuddly curious clever cool comfortable chair-hogger crazy (at times)…and completely cherished

awesome adorable alert adventurous acrobatic affectionate aggravating (once in a while)… but still absolutely angelic

tender tidy talented talkative treat-munching toy-chasing trained (not!)…and tremendously treasured

soft sweet special
spectacular swishy-tailed
snuggly spirited spunky
(Hey! Get down
from there!)…
and stupendously
spoiled

Cat and Mouse Maze Solution

Happy
is the
home
with
at least
one cat.

Proverb

"Parlor Cat" Design

Colored By: ______________________________

Date: ____________________________________

Amazing Pawsibilities!

As anyone who shares a home with a cat knows, a cat is happy to play with his toys, but not inclined to pick them up when he's finished. As you make your way through this maze, pick up each toy and the basket in the middle will be full!

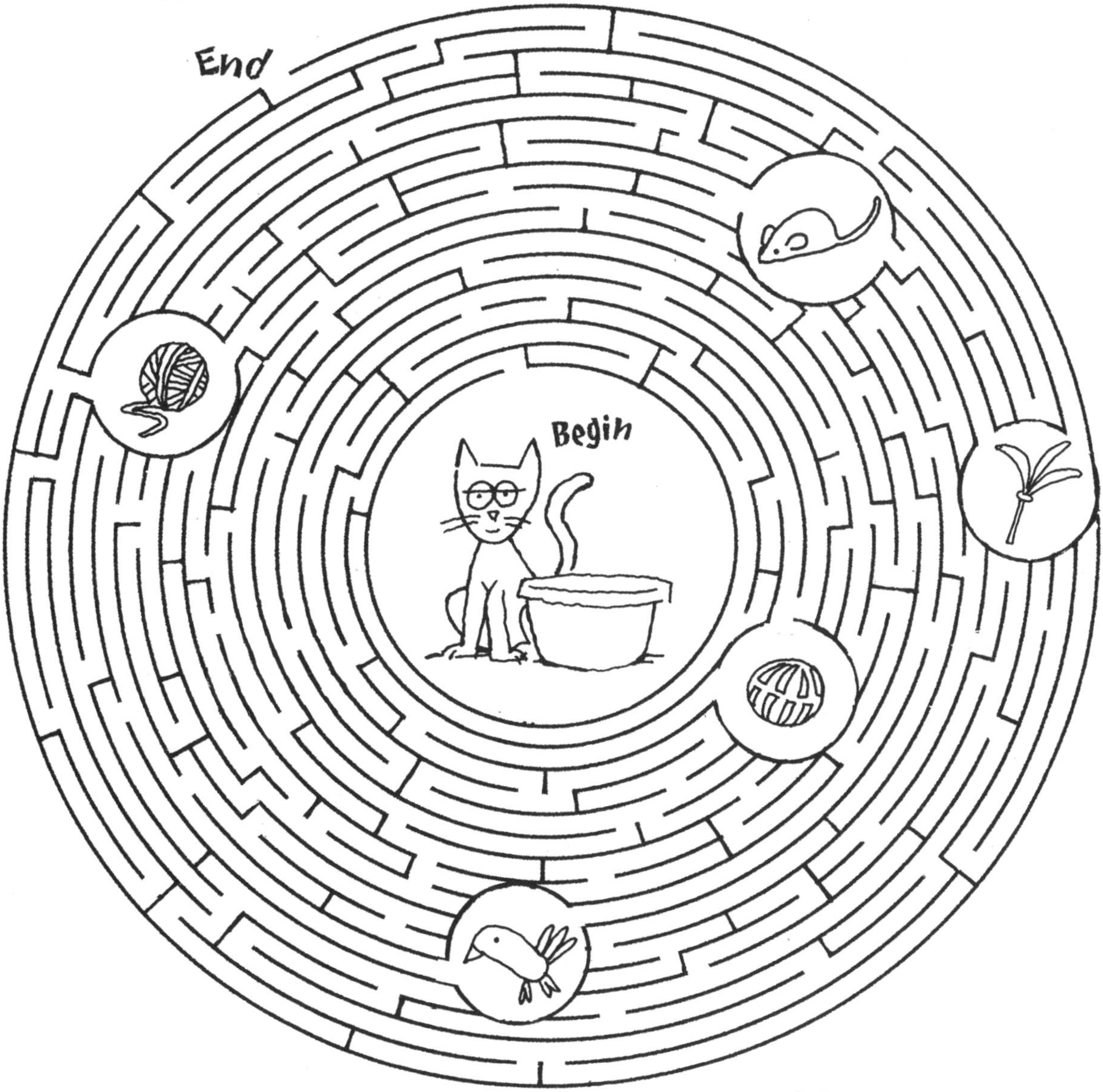

Solution on next page.

"While I was holding the cat,
someone started the vacuum cleaner."

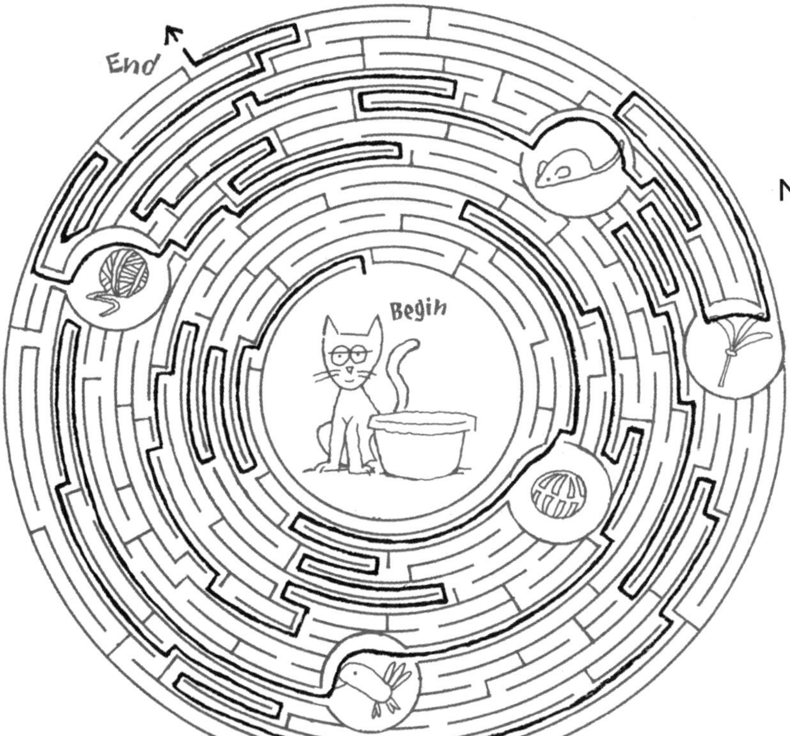

Maze Solution

If you don't
have anything
nice to say
about someone...
only tell
your cat
about it.

"Purrfect Patterns" Design

Colored By: ______________________________

Date: ______________________________

Katza Palooza! Draw, doodle, decorate delightful cats!

T-Shirt Retreat For Kitty

1. Select a cardboard box that a T-shirt will fit over snugly.

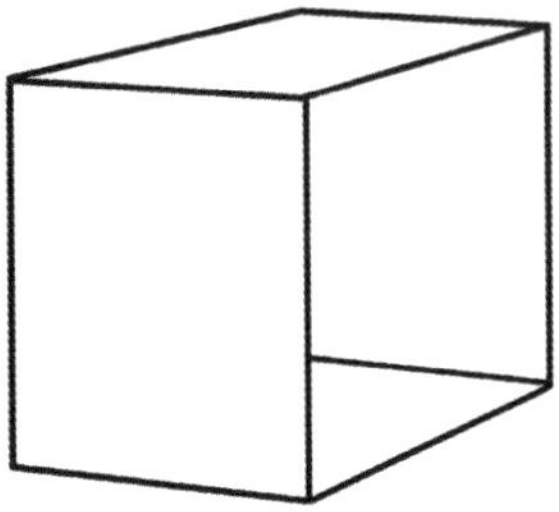

2. Ease the T-shirt over the box putting the neck hole in the center of the opening in the box.

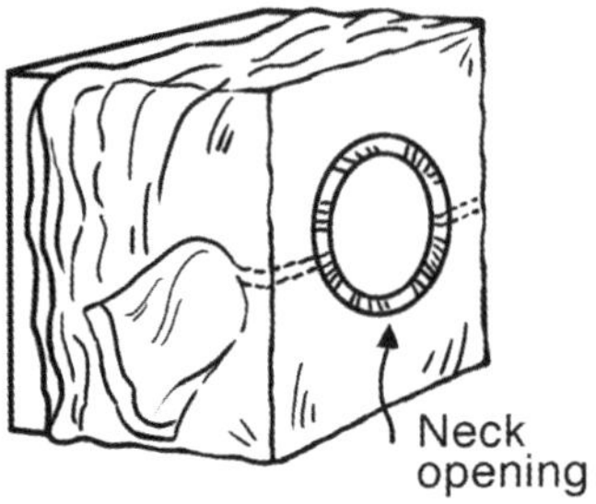

3. Twist and roll the two edges of the bottom of the shirt together. Tie the ends into a knot.

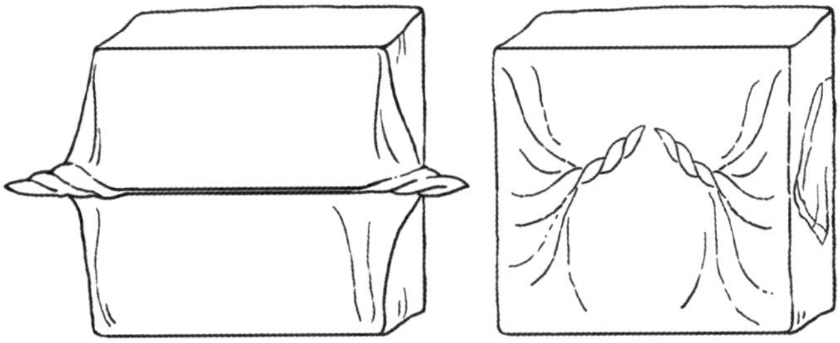

4. Hide the sleeves by tucking them into the shirt.

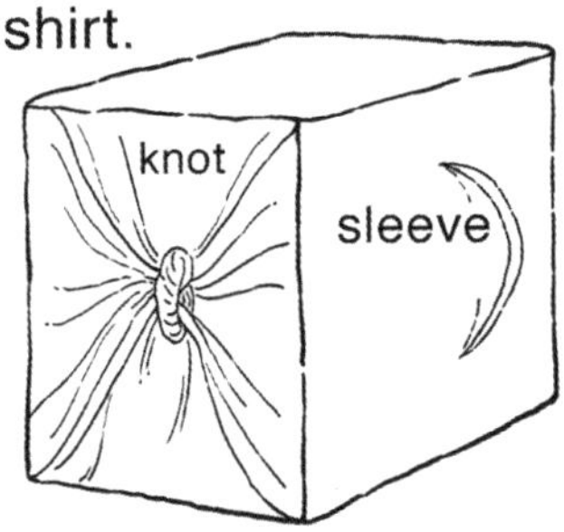

5. Put a towel inside the box through the open neck to make a bed.

Make a home for your kitten, and before you know it, the kitten has made a home in your heart!

Paws to Connect the Dots

Solution on next page.

Q: Where did the astronaut cat get her milk?
A: From flying saucers!

Q: What makes a cat in the desert like Christmas?
A: Its sandy claws!

Q: What kind of cats like to go bowling?
A: Alley cats!

Q: What do you call a cat that likes to lick lemons?
A: A sour puss!

Q: What did the feline Shakespearean actor say on stage?
A: Tabby or not tabby!

Q: Why wouldn't the cat go near the oak tree?
A: Because of its bark.

Paws to Connect the Dots Solution

Any thing
gets
better
with
enough
hugs.

"A Friend's Hug" Design

Colored By: ______________________

Date: ______________________

Spot the Hidden Cats!

In the drawing, see if you can locate all 14 kitties!

Solution on next page.

Hidden Cats Solution

The simplest pleasures mean the most.

"Barn Cat" Design

Colored By: ______________________________

Date: ___________________________________

Follow the color key on the back cover for this color-by-number design, or create your own original color scheme

DOODLE CATS

Design and decorate these cats in your own way.

How to Draw a Long Haired Cat

1. Create oval shapes to indicate the cat's shape.

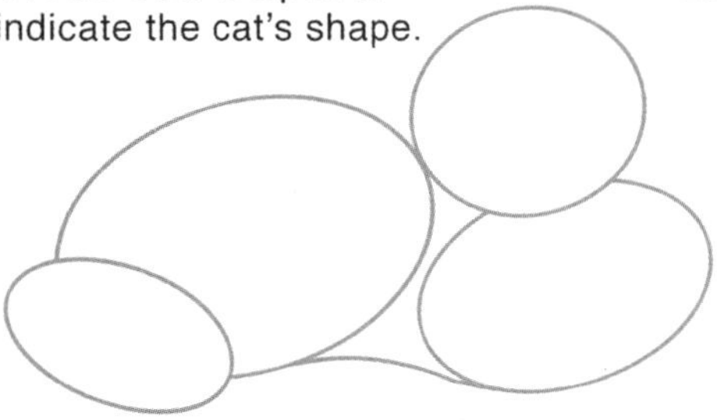

2. Add shapes for ears, eyes, face details, and indicate direction for legs and tail.

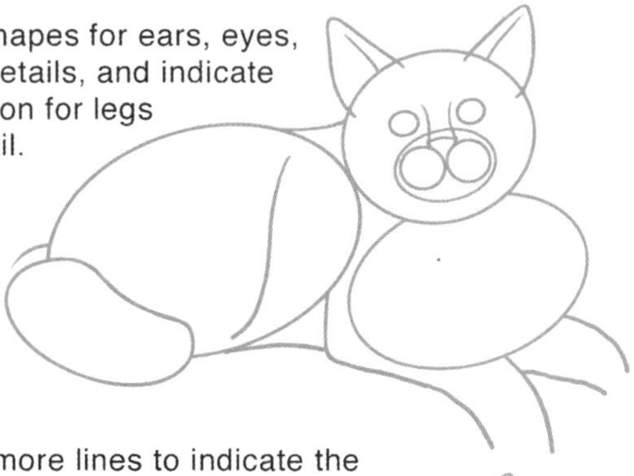

3. Add lines that indicate flow of cat's long fur. Indicate oval shapes for paws.

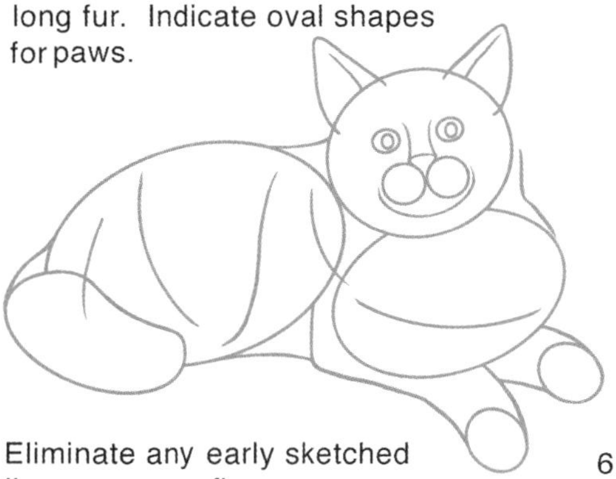

4. Add more lines to indicate the shape of fur. Refine the lines and shapes for the face and body.

5. Eliminate any early sketched lines as you refine your drawing.

6. For the finished cat, add patterns in the fur, whiskers, more details to make the cat look fluffy.

AlphaCats

Copy the AlphaCats on the next pages to create all kinds of fun.

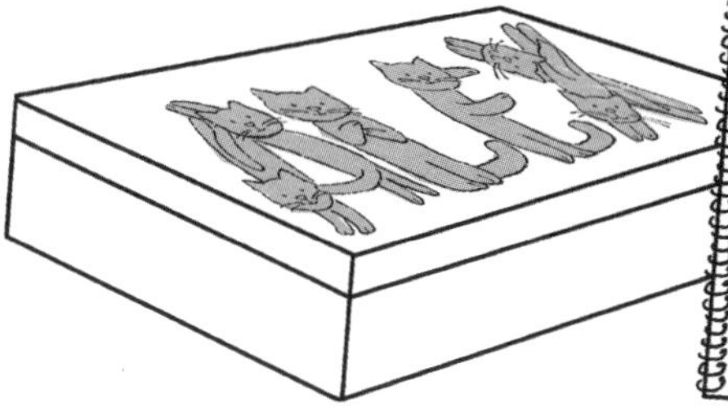

Decorate a room or a door sign.

Label your own stuff or personalize a gift for someone else.

Make a gift special.

Decorate a box or bin to hold things.

STUV
WXYZ

"Winter Window" Design

Colored By: ______________________________

Date: ______________________________

Follow the color key on the ba
cover for this color-by-number
design, or create your own
original color scheme.

FUN WITH HUMANS

WHEN YOUR HUMAN TRIES TO MAKE A BED, DO THIS . . .

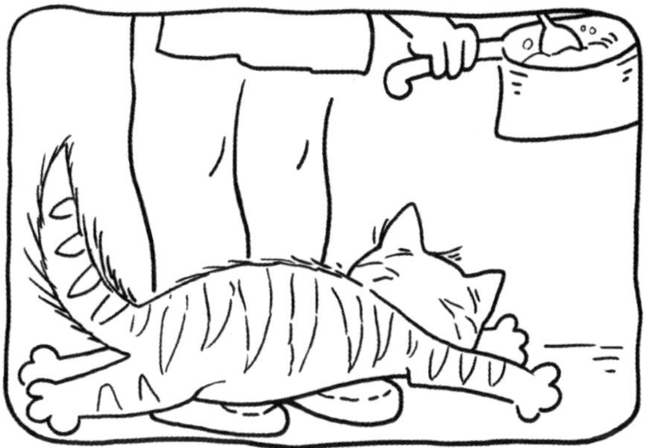

WHEN YOUR HUMAN IS TRYING TO COOK, DO THIS . . .

WHEN YOUR HUMAN WANTS TO READ, DO THIS . . .

WHEN YOUR HUMAN IS TRYING TO DO THE LAUNDRY, DO THIS . . .

WHEN YOUR HUMAN IS KNITTING, DO THIS . . .

WHEN YOUR HUMAN IS EXERCISING, DO THIS . . .

A Paws for Reflection

Be sure to find time to play...
Soak in the warmth of the sun...
Never lose your sense of curiosity...
Express yourself...
and remember
a thankful heart finds blessings every day.

The End

Happy tails to you!